Human Geographies

Calliope Chapbook Series

Megan Muthupandiyan

This collection of poems is a human-made work of imagination. No part of this book may be reproduced, distributed, or transmitted in any form or by any means without written permission of the publisher, except in the case of brief quotations used in a review of the book.

Human Geographies
© Megan Muthupandiyan, 2025
All rights reserved.

ISBN: 978-1-952526-26-8

Published in the United States
as a part of
Calliope Chapbook Series
a collaborative project with
Lakeland University's Literary Publishing class
Editors: Madeleine Wattenberg, Assistant Professor,
A. Yvonne Kumrow, Megan Hunt, and Jenna Winge

Water's Edge Press LLC
Tucson, Arizona

Cover image of Point du Cimetière provided by the author.
Cover and book design by Water's Edge Press LLC

NO AI TRAINING: Without in any way limiting the author's and publisher's exclusive rights under copyright, any use of this publication to "train" generative artificial intelligence (AI) technologies to generate text is expressly prohibited. The author reserves all rights to license uses of this work for generative AI training and development of machine learning language models.

For the one with whom
I am always gracelessly stumbling
into sacred woods.

Mallorca, 2017

N 39°29′33.14″ E 2°28′13.24″

El Toro

for Alex, Sina, and Sona

Time was the first windmill
to run into disuse;
I have seen
its ancient tower
lie all but abandoned,
a ruin of suggestion.

While night-swimming
a satellite sails low overhead,
a trow breaking
the crest of darkness;
elsewhere the world burns,
but we find it hard to remember.

Floating with arms outstretched
we catch the breath of night
and begin to circle
the summer constellations,
grinding coarse starlight
into the finest meal.

N 39°29′12.43″ E 2°28′30.77″

Port Adriano

Along the sea wall
the girls walk
as through shattered pottery,
avoiding the resurrection places
where the waters have evaporated
and minerals are spiriting
out of the volcanic stone.

Along the sea wall
the girls are
enmeshed in the elements;
unmoored by sea, unbound by sky
salt is a predator,
seizing light
with the same brilliance
it possesses as it wounds.

Elm Grove, 2022

N 42°2'43.15" W 83°4'41.83"

An Ancient Circle

One night,
        as the men
sleep beneath the boreal glow
of late-night television
and the women gather
around the fire,

                a game
of ghosts in the graveyard
dissolves
        when a son decides
to step into the cooler
to see how long he can bear the pain
of standing shin-deep
in crystalline cocktail ice.

And with that,
        an ancient circle re-forms;
the boys remove their shirts
and draw down their guns
to watch the rite,
each soundlessly
        awaiting his turn,
deep in the resolute night.

☾ 08ʰ18ᵐ30ˢ N 24°58'
♂ 08ʰ18ᵐ30ˢ N 21°12'

Viewing the Conjunction at Home

As the Moon and Mars
appulse like passing lovers
view their conjunction
without forgetting you're looking backwards.

The light has taken time to reach your eyes;
it always takes time to see two bodies
braced in closest separation
and know they remain light years apart.

Kyoto, 2024

N 35°00′7.80″ E 135°46′25.79″

朱色 Shuiro

朱
Shu

In six strokes 朱 takes form,
resembling this bird abode—
the sacred torii whose threshold
I have just stepped over
to enter the shrine grounds
as two Komadori perch upon it.

朱—

The kanji writes us, is not merely written—
the phoenix-fire of the gate
mirrored in toes painted vermillion,
blood orange hues reflecting
the brush of the birds' cinnabarine breasts
as they ink the sky with song.

色
iro

With six more strokes 色
is constructed and christened—
a little ship set sail on the sea of consciousness,
devoid of steerage and
stacked with conceptual freight.

Color, Kind, Lover, Appearance, Complexion, Type—
色 courses the trade winds of attention
with so many cargo boxes in its hold!

But in truth they are all hollow bellied—
iro is a container full of empty containers,
manned by only the captain, 朱.

N 34°58′1.00″ E 135°46′30.00″

The Torii Gates of Mount Inari

Erected one
        after another,
after another,
        after another,
with barely a hand's breadth
between them,
the torii gates of Mount Inari
leave pilgrims poised
on the threshold of paradox:
step through
        from this side to that side,
this way to that way,
        this world to the next,
pass into the infinite
by way of the infinitesimally small places
between us—
sacred spaces you will enter while departing,
moments yet to and already come.

Chicago, 2000 *and* 2018

N 41°52′38.10″ W 87°37′54.30″

Visiting the Chicago Board of Trade

As we watched the men and women brokering
futures on the exchange floor
of the Chicago Board of Trade
you carefully explained
the economics of speculation
while my attention drifted upward
to the vertical lines of the art deco skylights
that exploded like sun rays
above them, above us . . .
humans rapt in the enterprise
of drafting promises,
building relationships and binding commitments
with an eye to their projected value,
not yet feasting on their reward.

N 41°52'45.70" W 87°37'25.00"

In the Hall of Antiquities

In the Hall of Antiquities
an elderly couple stands
coupling as only mammals do—
tending to one another's bodies
in the places not easily reached.

Before the small bronze
of Dionysos and Ampelos
he has taken her woolen coat
and gloves to free her hands—
blanched linen, they course
like sails over his back,
the nails bobbing
along the rocky shoreline of his neck.

Oh God! Yes! he cries,
not in respectable, whisper filled sighs
but with bright exaltation—
an ecstasy born of pain, fulfilled in relief—
and the sound rises
like ceremonial smoke,
and is absorbed
by the statuary and metalwork—
not an echo has been forged.

As they move on
I draw nearer to the statue
of the god gazing
down into the eyes of
his beloved woodland satyr—
and my eyes gloss
over the detailed metalwork
of his sculpted face and tiny shoes,
rest instead
on the lovers' manicuring embrace.

How is it I've never seen
the way Ampelos is reaching toward
Dionysos' side to massage that
old war wound—
the way Dionysos scratches
Ampelos' strong stout shoulder?

The sight of these two lovers
leavening one another's discomfort . . .

it changes their patina,
their beauty, their value—
draws truth
from art,
it changes everything.

Paris, 2012

N 48°51'48.57" E 2°19'38.53"

Dans le Jardin du Carrousel

A Dionysian dusk pours over Paris,
possessing nothing
of Autumn's hesitation
as it flows over tourists leaving the Louvre,
lavishly drinks them up.

Through the sculptured hedges
my daughter and I
weave at the edge of darkness,
giggle-drunk with the furtive pleasure
of children who are hiding—

not lost, and yet, unfound.

N 48°43′29.00″ E 2°15′30.00″

À Massy Palaiseau

Farther down the platform
a woman stands
shrouded
within a black burqa,
a thin gold watch
shimmering on her wrist.

She may be the last word
the poet seeks—
her shifting shapelessness
strangely becoming,
a world
of intimation.

Ghana, 2024

N 5°37'24.43" W 0°10'44.33"

Finding Pothos

I. *Evergreene Palms, Accra, 2024*

Inside Gidi and Gladys's roadside nursery
the nineteenth century *L'Illustration horticole*
is drawn in life, each cultivar
of Jean Jules Linden and Édouard André's
horticultural expeditions
to South America and Oceania
potted in the colors of kente,
woven and rewoven by the grill-filtered light.

Set like a semicolon
among conflagrations of Bromelia
and bristles of Blood Banana
a Pothos leans in its azure pot;
planted in stone and staked with bamboo
it is a most modest vine, a mere seven leaves long,
each reaching out in a different direction
like arms shot through with veins of gold.

100 cedis; I pick it up—
the gift I sought at any cost.

> II. *La Sapienza, Roma, 1940*
>
> *. . . Although one is missing his head*
> *and both are missing their arms,*
> *the sculptures found in the viaduct beneath Via Cavour*
> *are essentially the same—*

*each leans so deep into the absence to his left
that his himatia has come undone
and hangs on his arm,
leaving his body as naked as his soul.*

*With a fat goose at their feet,
they both bear all the iconography
of Pothos—brother to Eros and Himeros—
the Greek daimon of a longing
that cannot be assuaged,
a distance that cannot be closed.*

*Notably, they seem to have been commissioned
for the same villa
during the Hadrianic Period;
standing side by side now,
as they were in the immutable dark
of the deep underground—
they are echoes of one another
and of some ancient love dispossessed . . .*

    III. *Guadalcanal, Solomon Islands, 1880*

    *Andrés taken to calling it the Devil's Ivy—
    the natives describe it as impossible to kill,
    evergreen through a seeming eternity of dark
    or drought,
    needing nothing to thrive, feeding on no more
    but mist.*

    *The creeping vine displays a perennial hunger—
    each heavily cuticled cordate leaf*

the size of a pauper's palm
cupped and begging at a passing carriage
as the other cleaves unsteadily to a post.

Ah, home—

But to the point, we've found it everywhere
and wonder at a suitable name—
growing thick in rain and cloud forests
of these islands, along the riparian floors,
mounting their ravines,
this plant does not develop
beyond the juvenile phase
unless cultivated with care;
no matter how earnestly it reaches,
unless terraced and trained
it is unable to secure itself to hosts.

IV. *Tetteh Quarshie Avenue, Accra, 2024*

As I hand him the potted plant
to climb into the car
I can tell by his face that being foreign
makes me quixotically charming.

Ghanian women of a certain age,
he explains,
want delicacies or fabric—
things to put out on the table for guests,
gifts to savor twice—
in receiving and in sharing.

As he puts the car into drive
the gold-rent leaves of the vine
surge to the left and I nod thoughtfully
at the tenderness of everything—
this tiny plant, this cultural logic,
the way he's explained it—
even while I am softened against doubt
that this Pothos I've found
will bring solace and joy
to the mother of my colleague in America,
a stranger whom I am about to meet.

To him I say nothing of this,
think nothing but this—

> *if you would take it and tend it,
>   I would give you this Pothos too.*

N 5°24′59.99″ W 1°18′60.00″

Kakum National Park

for Nabali, Nasiba, and Sammy

Some sixty meters high within this moist forest
the crowns of the Mahogany
and Kyenkyen trees spread like dendrites
separated by synapses of sky;
we move through its cerebral mantle
as evergreen, as ever, shy—
but there is, at last, no wanting.

As a butterfly flutters
past my face the small wind it makes invites
thought of fate, the faultless knowing
we have arrived at a place
where gentleness knows no season
and strength grows on nothing but atmosphere,
as epiphytic as the ivory orchids
arching over our heads.

I close my eyes to feel the sway
of the final bridge in Kakum
and all that separates us falls away;
somehow we have become one
with and within
this emerald organon,
this body of bodies in perennial bloom.

Langlade, 1997 *and* 2011

N 45°10′40.00″ W 88°43′23.93″

Sangsue

Mornings in March
find us in Old Man Lazarus's woods,
where the sugar maples grapple at the sky,
their arthritic limbs
stilled by that Rip-van-Winkling winter.

At sap collecting time
the fog curls lazily around his shoulder
as if it were a dear friend,
filling in the spaces between us
as he limps ahead
with his empty bucket of galvanized steel.

Small blue bags are strung up
across the trees like buoys warning
No Wake in fishing waters,
ballooning like the gullets of bullfrogs
we caught in mid-breath
summers before.

Reaching out to take one off
its silver spicket,
Lazarus's rheumatic hands
become an extension of the tree,
their sinewy knuckles lightly brushing
its bark in a circular motion
as he pours the clear liquid
from the bag into his pail.

"We are harvesting its blood," he says.

Standing stout on thickly bowed legs,
he laughs heartily,
his eyes disappearing
in the weathered folds of his face,
and as the grove echoes his voice
with its high-pitched mimicry
in the dull grey light
I am convinced that he was a misplaced tree,
uprooted and freed to wander.

Yet he never strays far,
wanting nothing except the pleasure of seeing
the expanding blue bags in the spring
and the special delicacy
of the cold, clear sap
that bleeds into them like sweet water;

the sap that he drinks
with closed eyes and a face of controlled joy.

N 45°8'18.87" W 88°37'57.69"

Becoming Irish

On the beach my son
buries his basalt skin
deep within
the white archipelagos
of sand,
becoming a rock—
uncharacteristically still.

"Don't you want to swim?"
I say, whispering
toward the steely water,
feeling my freckled back
begin its slow burn.

He shakes his head firmly
while pulling out
a chalky limb
tinctured with talcum—

"I'm too busy
becoming Irish."

Italy, 2003 *and* 2019

N 45°26'15.85" E 12°20'18.26"

Revisiting the Battlegrounds of Our Civil War

Like soldiers to the battlefield
whose events determined a war,
we returned after seven years
to this place
I had left, you crying.

Again we sought out
the oaken warmth of that same local pub—
L'Olandese Volonte,
                The Flying Dutchman,
and as you lit a cigarette,
I thought of that fabled ship
      denied entrance to any port,
doomed to pass into eternity
restless and searching on black waters.

Without speaking,
its crew scuttled below deck
throughout the dark galleys like beetles
scratching their only testament to their existence
on the ship's walls,
in words never to be read ...

                "We were here."

... "We were here," I said,
turning toward my husband—
you smiled and nodded in agreement
before your attention
was drawn away from
him and me
by a man who was harvesting laughter
from a crowd at the bar.

N 42°5′27.5″ E 12°24′6.90″

À Formello

for my daughter, for Gwa

The ridge across from your garden
falls as slowly as the final note
in the last lullaby I ever sang to her;
it bursts in violet stars of thistle
and comets of goldenrod—
the wild colors of a bicycle
she rides down the cobbles
of another village in another country.

Almost hidden from sight,
a farmer chugs along again in his harvester;
with the tilling and sowing completed
and the maturation and harvest yet to come,
all he can do is
survey the fields of his labor
each morning,
so he does.

Such is the landscape of love.

No matter where, with you
I stare out on this landscape;
it magnifies
the beauty of a child
without whom
beauty would have ever only been a word—
without whom this field
would have ever only been a field.

Senegal, 2024

N 14°40′4.50″ W 17°23′50.62″

At La Maison des Esclaves

    Before us
the curved staircases rise
between dungeons and heavens
like suppliant hands,
like DNA severed,
    shattered,
        broken.

    Within us,
everything is recombinant—
the architecture
    of this place
became the architecture
of our bodies,
    by design.

N 14°40′14.60″ W 17°23′57.80″

To Make Goree a UNESCO Site

Empty the prison,
transfer all the island's convicts to offshore cells—

Half-bury the old cannon fodder
to evoke a treasure waiting to be discovered, recovered ...
compel those locals to hang their laundry somewhere else—

Civilize the prison's, no, *fort's*, native black stone—
bring back that striking Portuguese vermillion—
saturate the walls until they bleed that blood red-orange—

Then a certain sort of perspective needs to be engineered,
of course—plant something tall and stately at the fort,
no, *museum's*, door—a snare of some barbed American cultivar
to deter or restrain those who might want to stray.

And it's imperative at last that the maps label this memorial
Point du Nord rather than *Point du Cimetière*—witnesses need
not know where the living and dead have been thrown.

Spain, 2012 *and* 2014

N 42°48′27.90″ W 7°36′55.87″

Above Portomarin

The trail flows deep
        until it stills,
dammed by a cairn
        of letters and photos,
strings and shoes,
all matter of things
left
        and lost

              and scattered
amidst the stone.

We step cautiously
where the roadside altar
overflows,
riffling into whirlpools
        of memory and desire
wanting to protect
the geology of places
where people
        have given
their wounds form.

N 42°52'27.90" W 8°33'1.36"

Santiago de Compostela

After the drunken man
is carried off the train
it continues its blind climb
into the night—

swaying unsteady
the hand of the poet,
unsure of the path
of her words
in the dark.

Coda

N 0°0′00″ E 0°0′00″

Nowhere

Against the wall
an old woman squats
threading marigold blossoms
on a string,
unaware of the
white cord of cloud
passing through the rays
of the orange sun.

We are always nowhere
other than the *there*
formed in *this*—
the cadence of images
giving rise to a song.

Acknowledgments

"Visiting the Chicago Board of Trade," "In the Hall of Antiquities," and "À Formello" first published in *Of the Earth and Other Desires: A Poet's Phenology*. League of Minnesota Poets Press, 2024.

"À Massy Palaiseau" and "Santiago de Compostela" first published as "Gares Poétiques/Estaciones Poéticas/Poetic Stations" in *Panorama: The Journal of Travel, Place and Nature*. Volume 10, Spring 2024.

About the Author

Photo by S. Muthupandiyan

Megan Muthupandiyan is a pilgrim, poet, and public humanities scholar who is most at home when she is walking the world. The founding director of Poetry in the Parks (poetryintheparks.org), much of her creative enterprise as an illustrator, poet, and essayist celebrates how individuals' participation in their land communities fosters their ecological consciousness.

Meg's poems, illustrations, photographs, and nature essays have appeared in over thirty journals and anthologies. She has authored two volumes of poetry, including *Forty Days in the Wilderness, Wandering* (Finishing Line Press, 2021) and *Of the Earth and Other Desires* (League of Minnesota Press, 2024), the winner of the 2023 John Rezmerski Manuscript Award.

To find out more about her work, please visit her portfolio at meganmuthupandiyan.com.

www.ingramcontent.com/pod-product-compliance
Lightning Source LLC
Chambersburg PA
CBHW030533080526
44586CB00011B/426